SECOND EDITION

Listen Here
songs by Dave Frishberg

piano • vocal • guitar

Photos by Owen Carey

ISBN 0-7935-4060-7

HAL•LEONARD®
CORPORATION

7777 W. BLUEMOUND RD. P.O. BOX 13819 MILWAUKEE, WI 53213

Visit Hal Leonard Online at
www.halleonard.com

It's difficult to find a category for Dave Frishberg's songs. The New York Times described him as "the Stephen Sondheim of jazz songwriting", and the London Daily Telegraph called him "a Woody Allen of song." The songs are carefully designed pieces that are often wryly amusing, occasionally tender and bittersweet, and sometimes contain pointed observations about American culture and values, and characterizations of people we all seem to know. "Although I sometimes think of them as cartoons, they are songs for adults," Frishberg says, "or at least for audiences that wouldn't mind growing up."

Long known as one of the outstanding pianists in jazz, Frishberg has since the early 1980s established himself as an internationally recognized composer and lyricist, as well as a solo performer with a loyal following.

After he left his home town of St. Paul, Minnesota, he became a busy pianist during the 1960s in New York City, playing regularly with the major jazz artists of the time, including Ben Webster, Al Cohn, Zoot Sims, Bobby Hackett, and Gene Krupa. As a singers' accompanist, he played for such diverse stylists as Carmen McRae, Dick Haymes, Anita O'Day, and Irene Kral. In 1971 he moved to Los Angeles where he worked as a studio musician, continued to write songs, and began to make records as a featured artist.

Four of his albums have won GRAMMY® nominations for best jazz vocal. His piano work is featured on recordings by Manhattan Transfer, Jimmy Rushing, Herb Alpert, Bill Berry's LA Band, Bud Freeman, Susannah McCorkle, and many other jazz and pop artists. Other artists who have recorded Frishberg songs include Ms. McCorkle, Rosemary Clooney, Michael Feinstein, Cleo Laine, Blossom Dearie, Carol Sloane, Mel Tormé, Diana Krall and Tony Bennett. Thanks to his widely heard recordings, and his appearances on *The Tonight Show*, *CBS Sunday Morning*, and public radio's *A Prairie Home Companion* and *Fresh Air*, Frishberg has become an increasingly familiar figure as a solo performer at festivals and clubs, on cabaret stages, and in concert halls in America and abroad. His songs, including the well-known "I'm Just a Bill", appear regularly on ABC's popular *Schoolhouse Rock* series. The reader will find several baseball-related songs in this collection. "I don't follow current baseball," Frishberg explains, "but I'm still hung up on the history of the game. I couldn't tell you who played in last year's World Series, but if you want to talk about Chet Laabs or Elbie Fletcher, we can do that." Since 1986, Frishberg has made his home in Portland, Oregon.

CONTENTS

Listen Here
songs by **Dave** **Frishberg**

ANOTHER SONG ABOUT PARIS

Words and Music by
DAVE FRISHBERG
Arranged by DAVE FRISHBERG

Lov-ers in the rain and flow-ers in the stall, on the Rue Ma-de-leine near the
Pi-geons on the grass on the Rue Souf-flot and pi-geons un-der glass at the

Place Pi-galle, how a-mus-ing when the gyp-sies stole our
Deux Ma-gots, how con-fus-ing when we could-n't find Mont-

wine. Re-mem-ber No-tre Dame, where we
martre. Re-mem-ber the small ho-tel where we

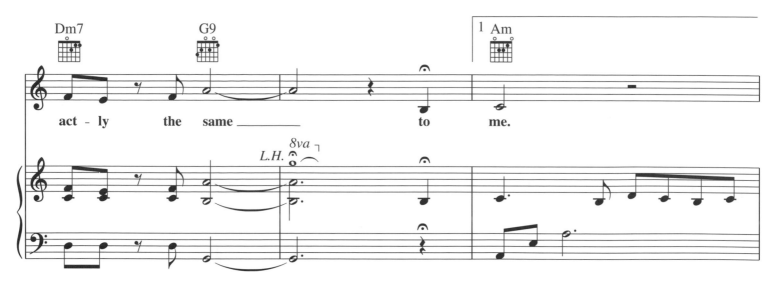

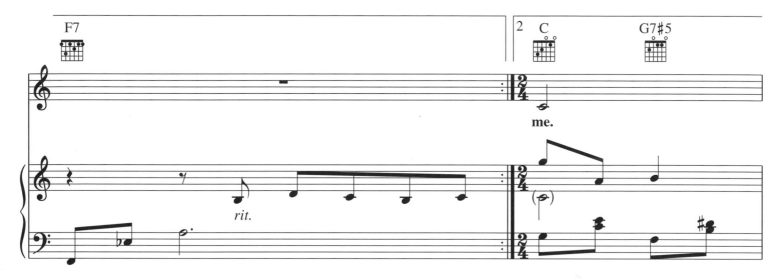

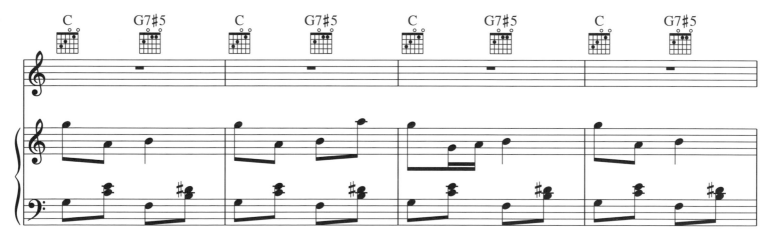

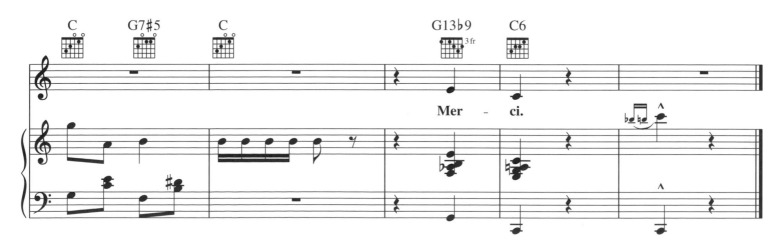

BLIZZARD OF LIES

Words and Music by DAVE FRISHBERG
and SAMANTHA FRISHBERG
Arranged by DAVE FRISHBERG

Moderately

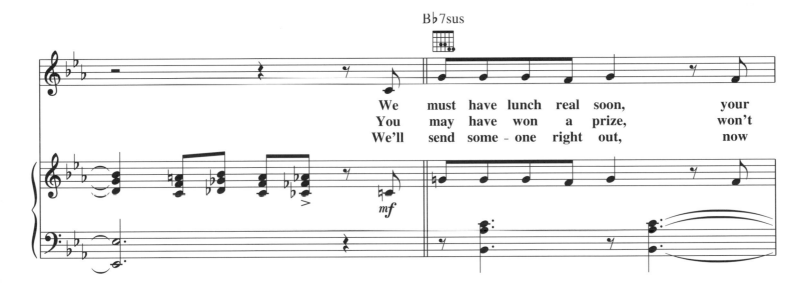

We must have lunch real soon, your
You may have won a prize, won't
We'll send some-one right out, now

lug - gage is checked through, we've
wrin - kle, shrink, or peel, your
this won't hurt a bit, he's

CAN'T TAKE YOU NOWHERE

Music by TINY KAHN and AL COHN
Words by DAVE FRISHBERG
Arranged by DAVE FRISHBERG

take you no-where. No, __ I can't __ take you no-where. I don't

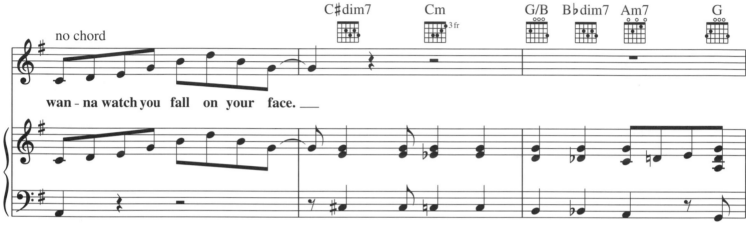

wan-na watch you fall on your face. __

You're __ take you no-where.

That's right! Try not to get up-tight. __
way. So have a real nice day." __

DEAR BIX

Words and Music by
DAVE FRISHBERG
Arranged by DAVE FRISHBERG

So, do what you got to do___ and may the years be good to you, ___ 'cause you're one of the fa-vored few, dear Bix, you're one of a kind.

THE DEAR DEPARTED PAST

Words and Music by
DAVE FRISHBERG
Arranged by DAVE FRISHBERG

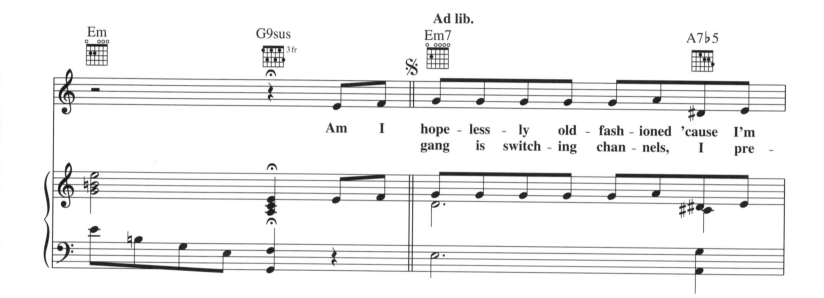

Am I hope-less-ly old-fash-ioned 'cause I'm
gang is switch-ing chan-nels, I pre-

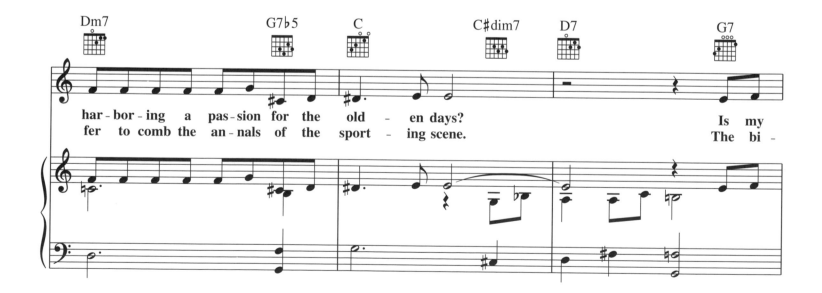

har-bor-ing a pas-sion for the old-en days?
fer to comb the an-nals of the sport-ing scene.

Is my
The bi-

Here's to the ways we'll see no more, the man-ner and the style that makes you want to
Here's to the clothes we used to wear, now, don't for-get your tie, and but-ton up your

smile in hap-py ret-ro-spec - tion. As for me, I don't think a-bout the
fly, and fas-ten your sus-pend - ers. As for me, I don't think a-bout to-

fu - ture, 'cause the fu - ture fades a-way too fast, and now's the time to
mor - row, 'cause to-mor-row was-n't built to last, and now's the time to

lift a cup of cheer and say, "Hear, hear," for the dear de-part-ed past.
weep a lit-tle tear in-to your beer for the dear de-part-ed past.

1 Bb7   Ebmaj7   **2** Bbmaj7   Cm7   Dm7   Ebmaj7   Dm7   G7

D.S. al Coda

While the

ad lib.

Brisk march

CODA   F7sus   Bb7   Eb   Eb7   Am7b5

hit - ter.

Three   cheers   for   the
Here's   to   the

D7#9   Gm   Fm7   Bb7

champs   of   yes - ter - day!   Jack   Demp - sey, John   Mc-
teams   that moved   a - way   from   dis - en - fran - chised

Eb   G7   Cm

Graw,   Joe   Lou - is, Sam - my Baugh,   the
towns,   the   old   Saint Lou - is Browns,   the

Slow, reflective

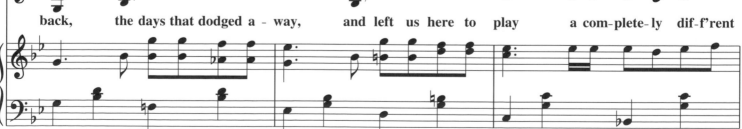

THE DIFFICULT SEASON

Words and Music by
DAVE FRISHBERG
Arranged by DAVE FRISHBERG

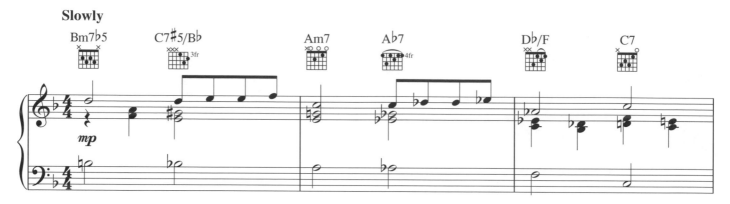

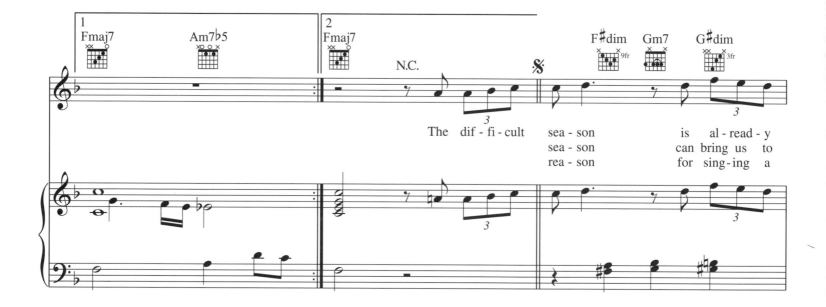

The dif - fi - cult sea - son   is al - read - y
sea - son   can bring us to
rea - son   for sing - ing a

here a - gain.   Deep in No - vem - ber each year   it starts to ap -
tears too much,   touch - ing on feel - ings and fears   too ten - der to
lone - ly song.   Ev - 'ry De - cem - ber it seems   the blues is our

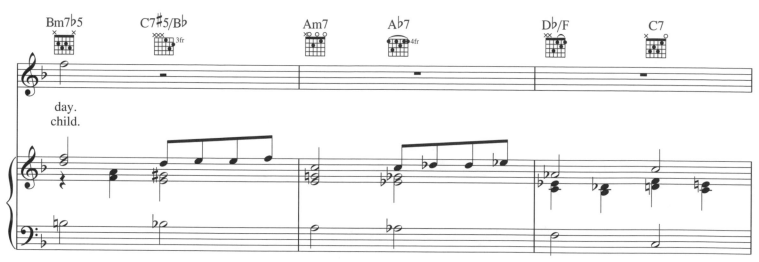

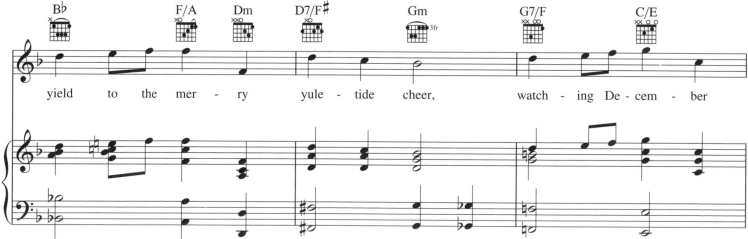

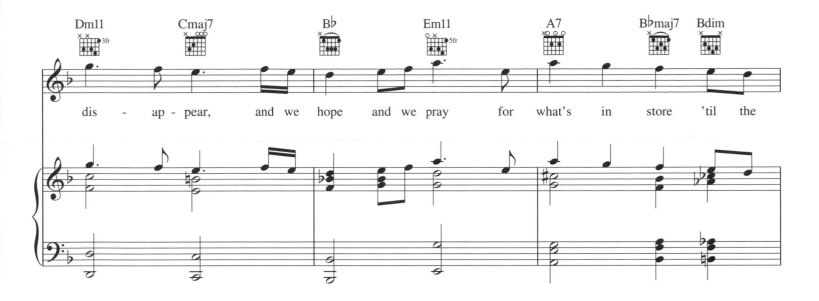

dis - ap - pear, and we hope and we pray for what's in store 'til the

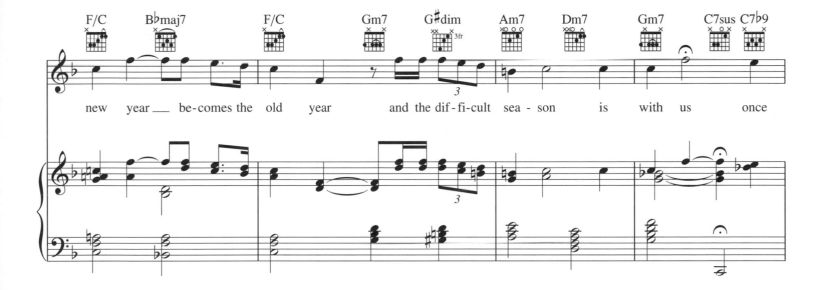

new year ___ be-comes the old year and the dif-fi-cult sea - son is with us once

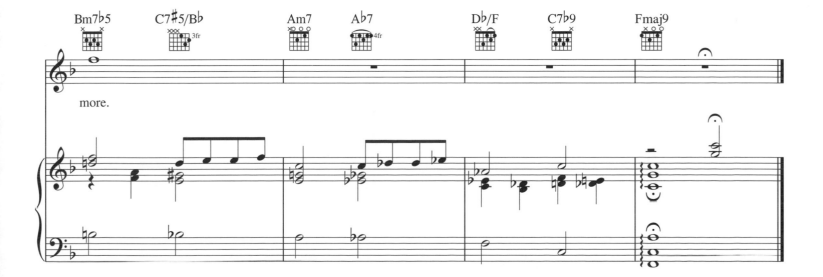

more.

DO YOU MISS NEW YORK?

Words and Music by
DAVE FRISHBERG
Arranged by DAVE FRISHBERG

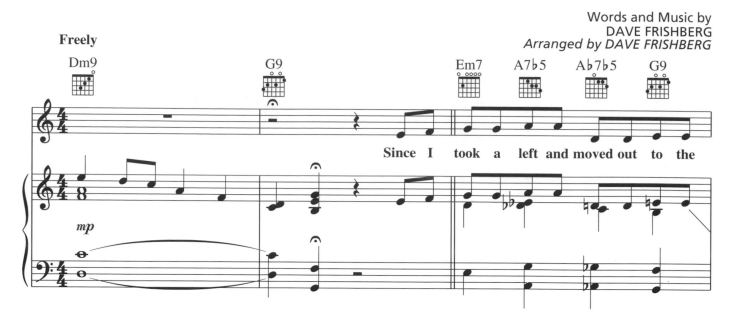

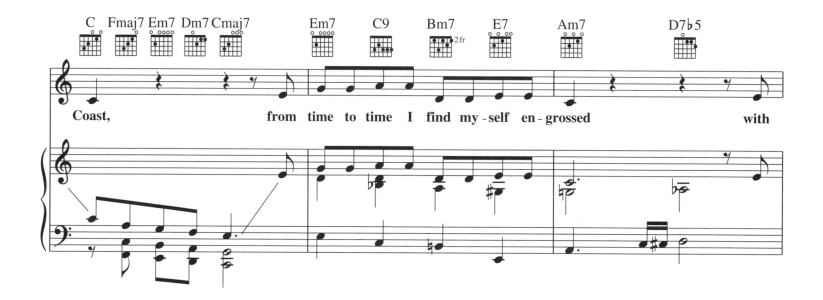

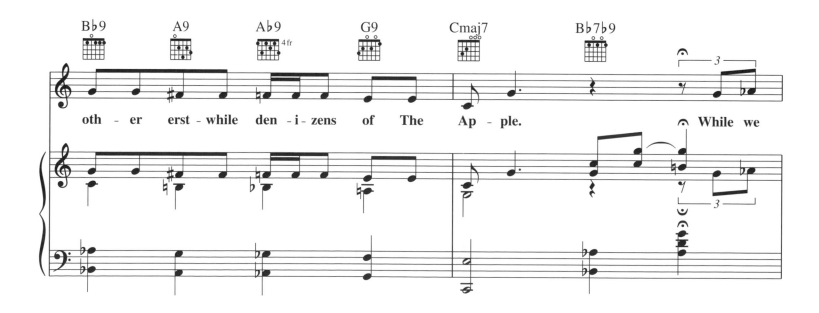

sit a - round and take L. A. to task,

there's a ques-tion some-one's bound to ask, and with this com-plex ques-tion we must

grap - ple.

Ballad, not too slow (♩ = 72)

Do you miss New York, the an - ger, the
Do you miss the strain, the traf - fic, the

DODGER BLUE

Words and Music by
DAVE FRISHBERG
Arranged by DAVE FRISHBERG

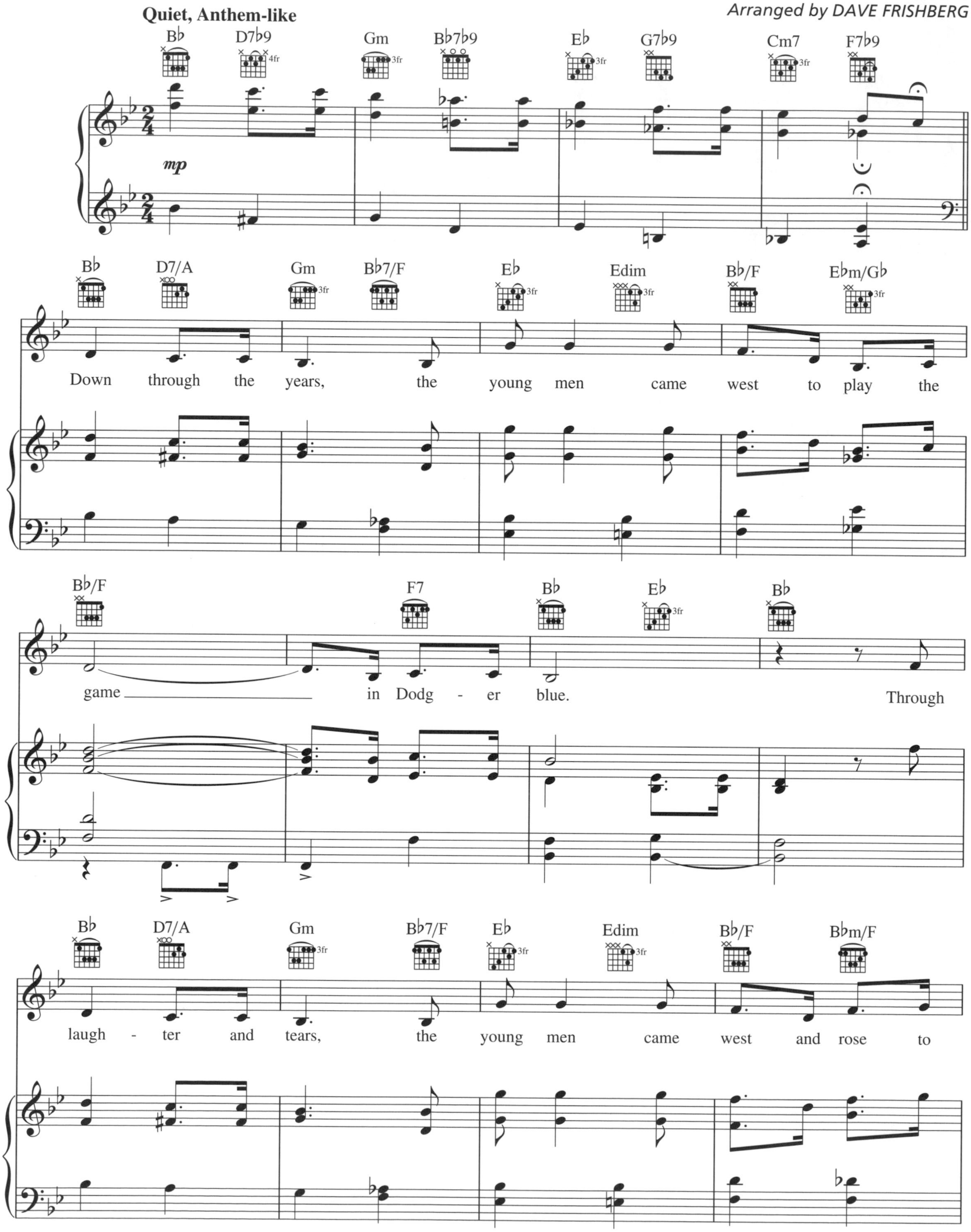
Quiet, Anthem-like
B♭ D7♭9 Gm B♭7♭9 E♭ G7♭9 Cm7 F7♭9
mp
B♭ D7/A Gm B♭7/F E♭ Edim B♭/F E♭m/G♭
Down through the years, the young men came west to play the
B♭/F F7 B♭ E♭ B♭
game in Dodg - er blue. Through
B♭ D7/A Gm B♭7/F E♭ Edim B♭/F B♭m/F
laugh - ter and tears, the young men came west and rose to

others stayed for man-y a sea-son through, but they all had a dream, and they all made the team, and they all wore Dodg-er blue. Mau-ry

Ballad tempo

Wills, Jim Fair-ey, Norm and Lar-ry Sher-ry, *Le-feb-vre, La-sor-da, and Val-en-tine, Reese and Rei-ser, and

*pronounced "la-fee-ver"

ELOISE

Words and Music by
DAVE FRISHBERG
Arranged by DAVE FRISHBERG

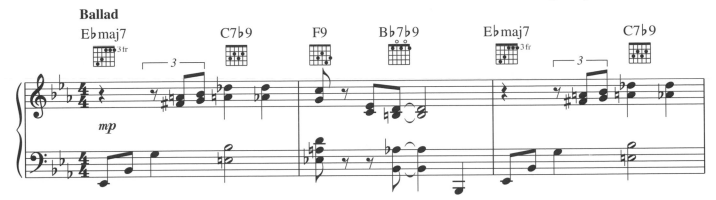

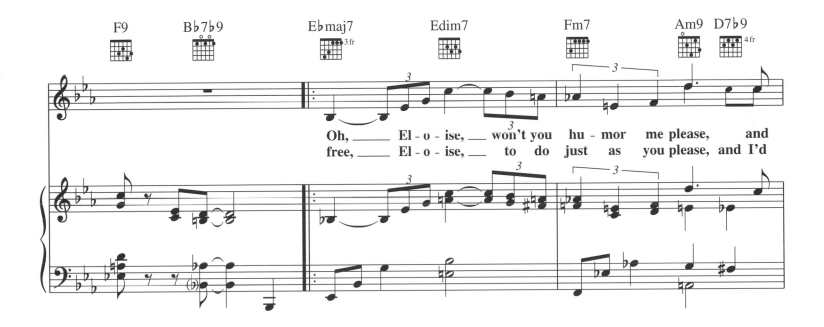

Oh, _____ El-o-ise, _____ won't you hu-mor me please, and
free, _____ El-o-ise, _____ to do just as you please, and I'd

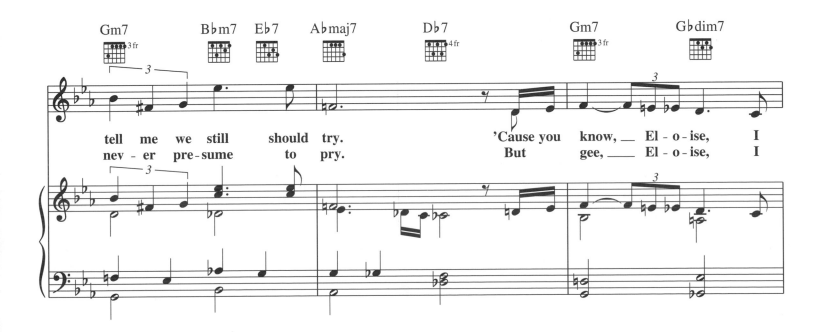

tell me we still should try.
nev-er pre-sume should to pry.

'Cause you know, _____ El-o-ise, I
But gee, _____ El-o-ise, I

EASTWOOD LANE

Words by DAVE FRISHBERG
Music by DAN BARRETT
Arranged by DAN BARRETT

Reflectively

Moderately slow

When the blue-bird __ in the church-yard __ starts to chirp, chirp, chirp __ in the rain, that bird sings mel-o-dies that car-ry me to my i-mag-i-nar-y home down in East-wood Lane. When the

* Vocal written one octave higher than sung.

GOTTA GET ME SOME ZZZ

Words and Music by
DAVE FRISHBERG
Arranged by DAVE FRISHBERG

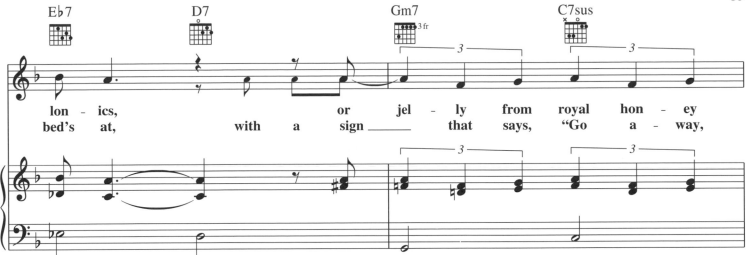

lon - ics,
bed's at,

or jel - ly from royal hon - ey
with a sign ____ that says, "Go a - way,

bees.
please.

I got to get me some zzz. ___
This man is get - ting some zzz." _

___
___

I don't need no Tur - kish bath or
I peek in the mirror, my face is

sau - na.
fro - zen,

I don't want no pills from no M.
like a guy who's dy - ing by de -

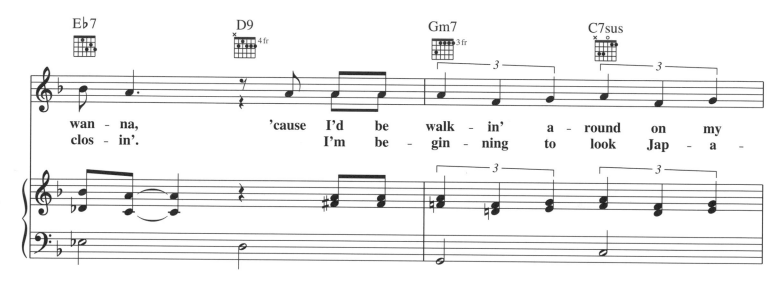

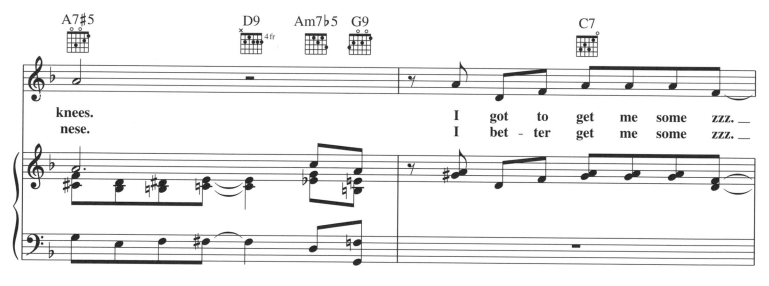

I WANT TO BE A SIDEMAN

Words and Music by
DAVE FRISHBERG
Arranged by DAVE FRISHBERG

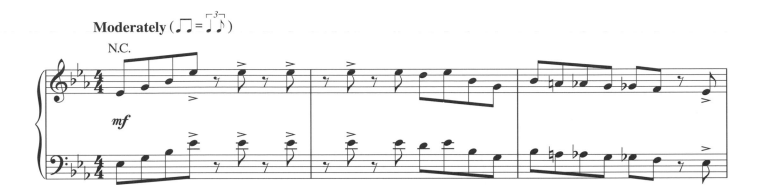

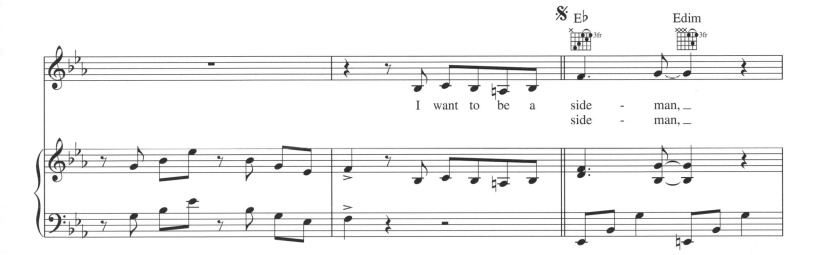

I want to be a side - man, __
side - man, __

just an or - di - na - ry side - man, __ a go a - long for the ride __
just a high - ly qual - i - fied man, __ a pro - fes - sion - al pride __

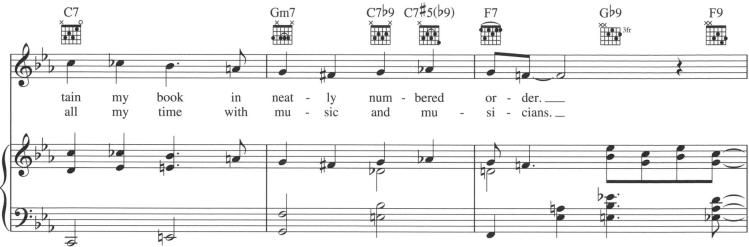

tain my book in neat-ly num-bered or - der. ___
all my time with mu - sic and mu - si - cians. ___

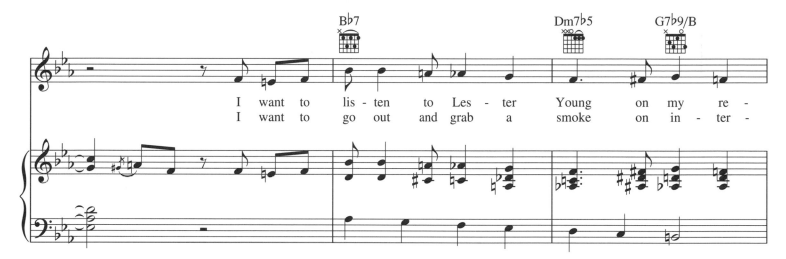

I want to lis - ten to Les - ter Young on my re -
I want to go out and grab a smoke on in - ter -

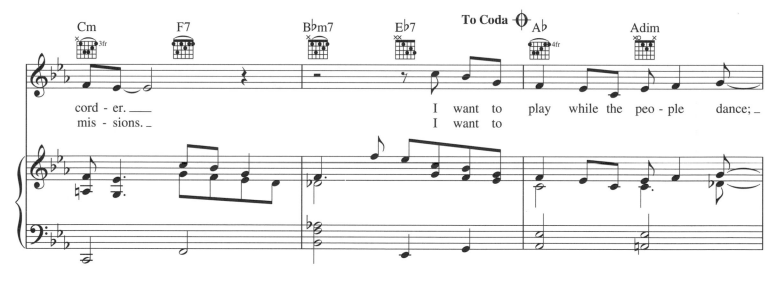

cord - er. ___ I want to play while the peo - ple dance; ___
mis - sions. ___ I want to

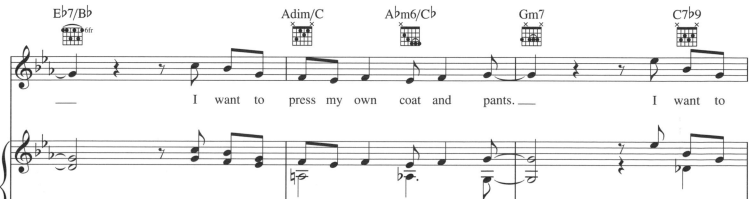

___ I want to press my own coat and pants. ___ I want to

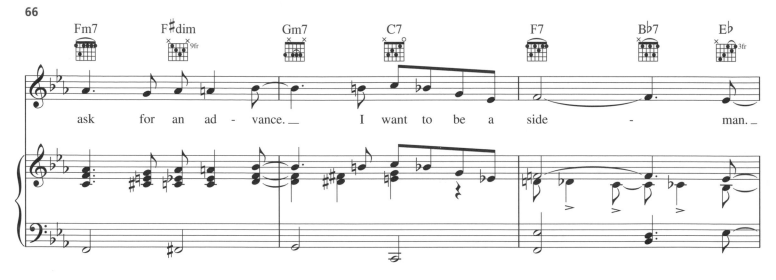

ask for an ad - vance. ___ I want to be a side - man. ___

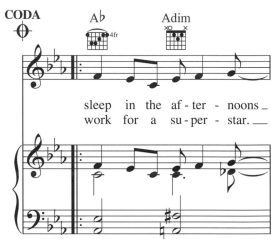

N.C. / D.S. al Coda / CODA / A♭ / Adim

___ I want to be a / sleep in the af - ter - noons ___ / work for a su - per - star. ___

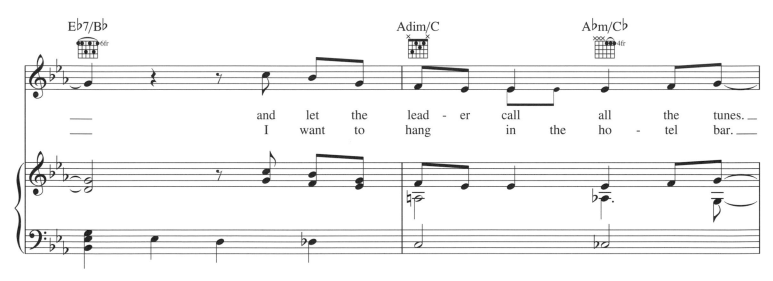

___ and let the lead - er call all the tunes. ___ / ___ I want to hang in the ho - tel bar. ___

___ I want to be young. I want to have fun. I want to be a / ___ I want to be

side - man. ___ I want to young.

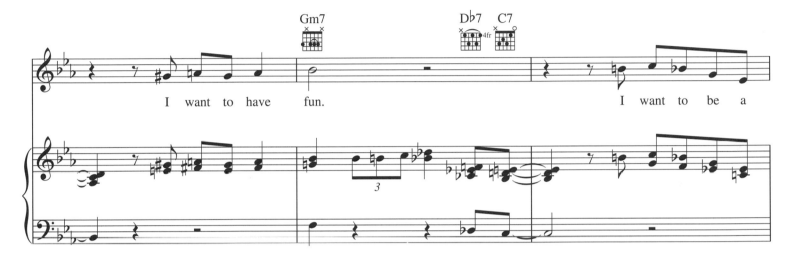

I want to have fun. I want to be a

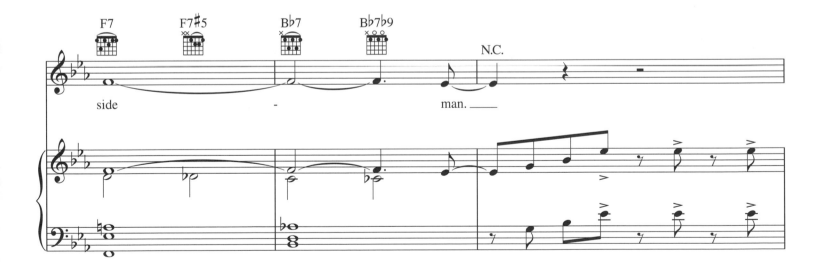

side - man. ___

HEART'S DESIRE

Words by DAVE FRISHBERG
Music by ALAN BROADBENT
Arranged by ALAN BROADBENT

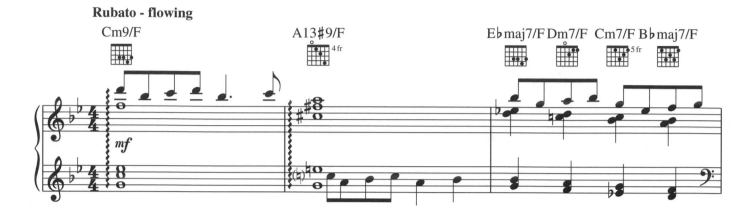

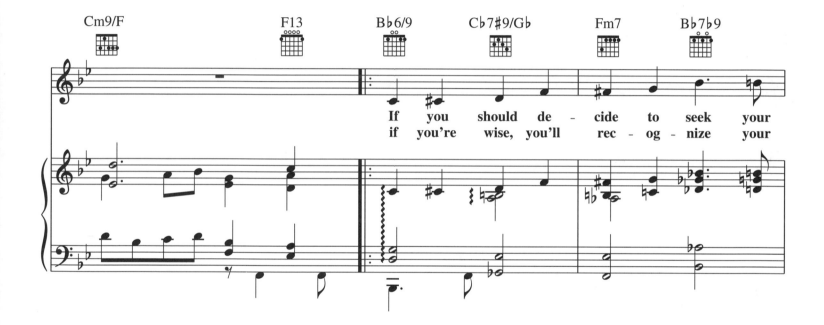

THE HOPI WAY

Words and Music by
DAVE FRISHBERG
Arranged by DAVE FRISHBERG

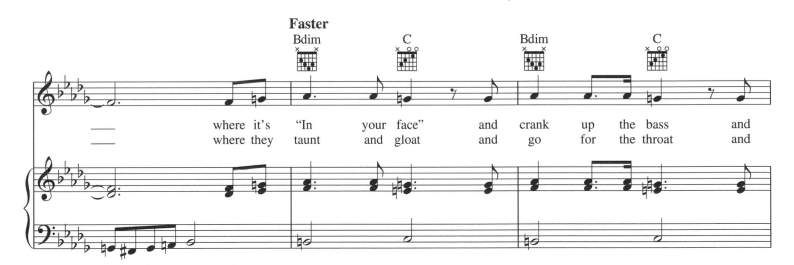

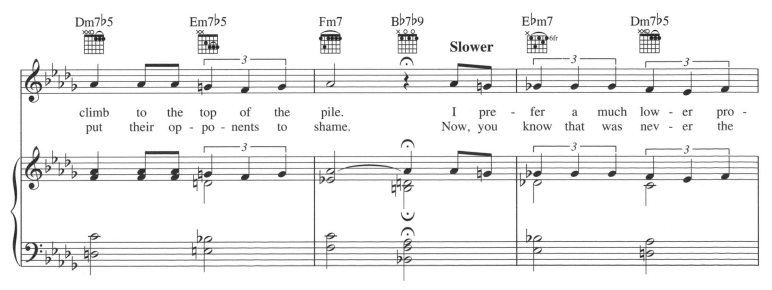

I WAS READY

Words and Music by
DAVE FRISHBERG
Arranged by DAVE FRISHBERG

I was read-y like a
read-y like a

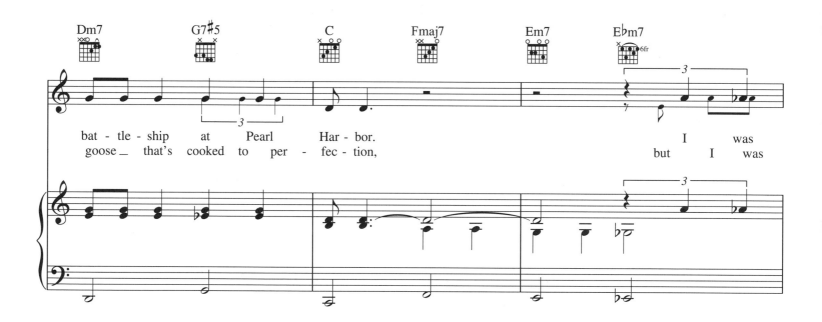

bat - tle - ship at Pearl Har - bor.   I was
goose __ that's cooked to per - fec - tion,   but I was

stead - y   like a shave with a part - time bar - ber.
o - pen   for a left to the low mid - sec - tion.

I'M HIP

Words by DAVE FRISHBERG
Music by BOB DOROUGH
Arranged by BOB DOROUGH

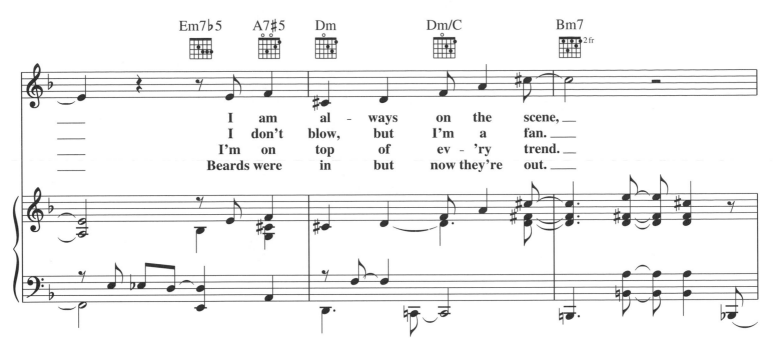

MARILYN MONROE

Words by DAVE FRISHBERG
Music by ALAN BROADBENT
Arranged by ALAN BROADBENT

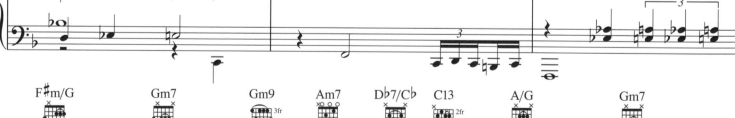

JAWS

Words and Music by
DAVE FRISHBERG
Arranged by DAVE FRISHBERG

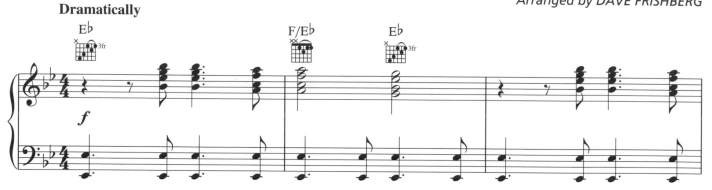

Jaws,
Jaws,

why are you drop - ping in dis - be - lief?   Tell me,
why are you gap - ing in shocked sur - prise?   Tell me,

LET'S EAT HOME

Words and Music by
DAVE FRISHBERG
Arranged by DAVE FRISHBERG

I like to dine in a Flo-ren-tine* pa-laz-
I like to eat in my suite at the Sa-voy Pla-

-zo; you can laugh and call me fat-
-za, and I know a bar in Ga-

-so. That's o-kay by me.
-za where they serve goat lip tea.

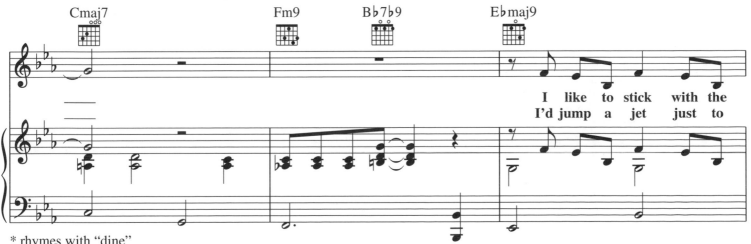

I like to stick with the
I'd jump a jet just to

* rhymes with "dine"

LISTEN HERE

Words and Music by
DAVE FRISHBERG
Arranged by *DAVE FRISHBERG*

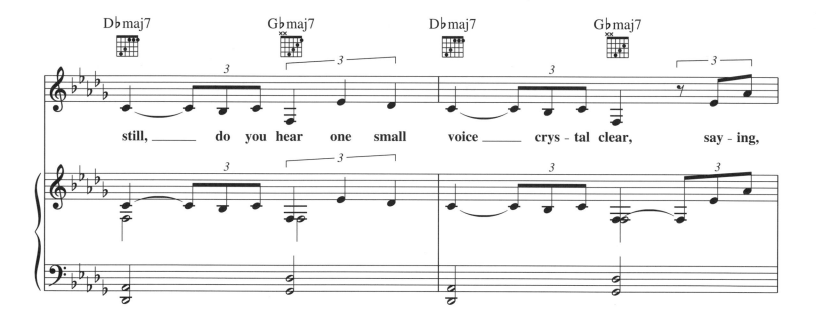

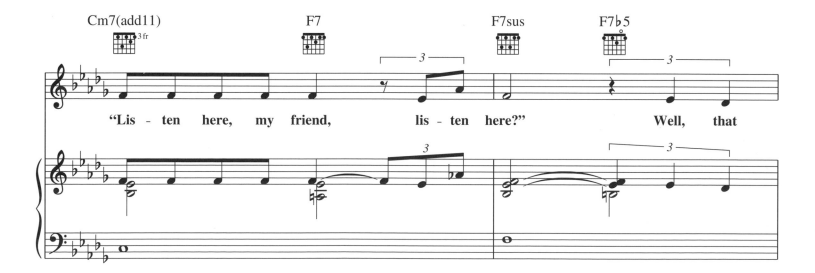

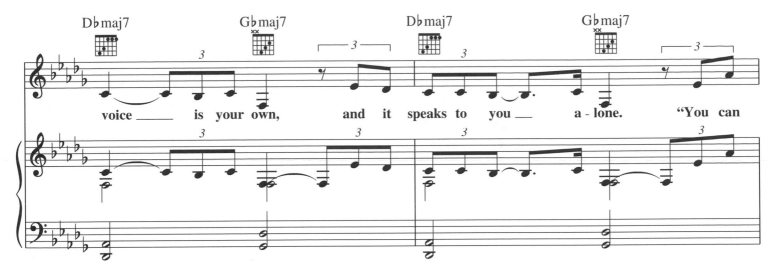

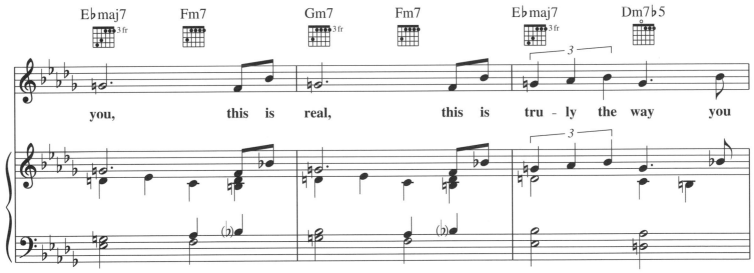

LITTLE DID I DREAM

Words by DAVE FRISHBERG
Music by JOHNNY MANDEL
Arranged by JOHNNY MANDEL

LOOKIN' GOOD

Words and Music by
DAVE FRISHBERG
Arranged by DAVE FRISHBERG

MATTY

(For Christy Mathewson, New York Giants 1900-1916)

Words and Music by
DAVE FRISHBERG
Arranged by DAVE FRISHBERG

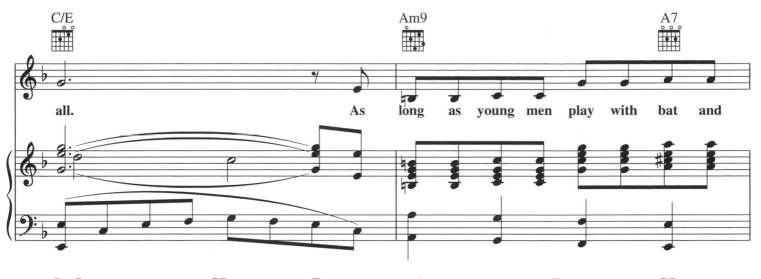

all. As long as young men play with bat and

ball, they'll tell of you, Mat - ty. ___ They'll re - mem - ber

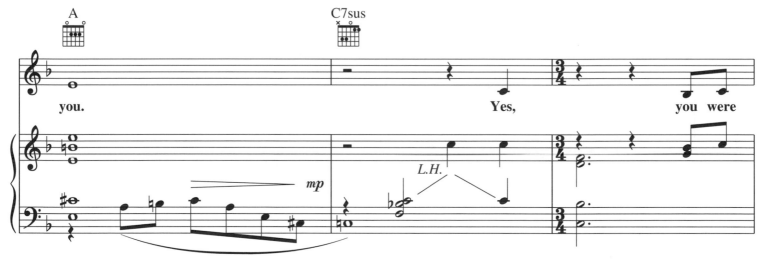

you. Yes, you were

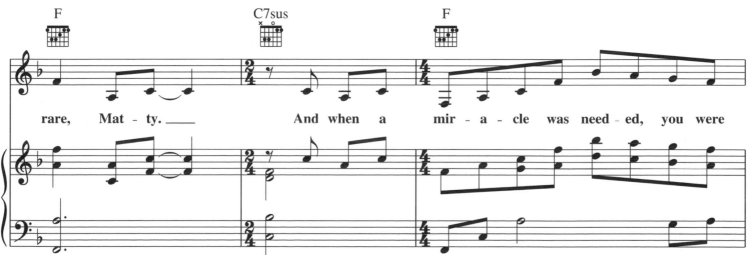

rare, Mat - ty. ___ And when a mir - a - cle was need - ed, you were

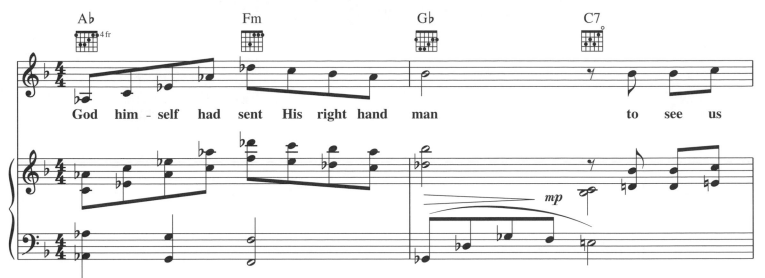

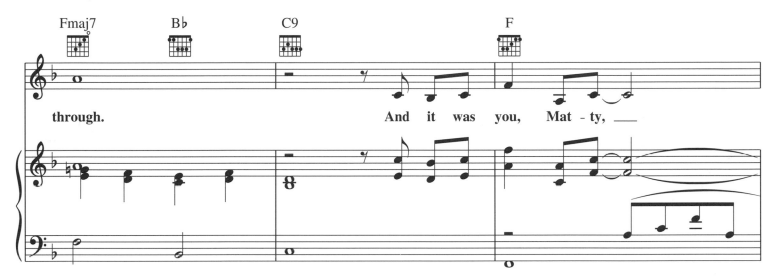

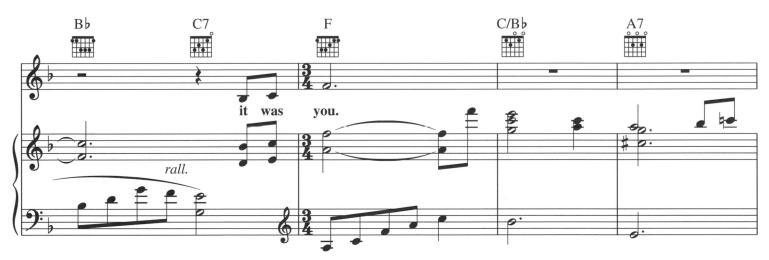

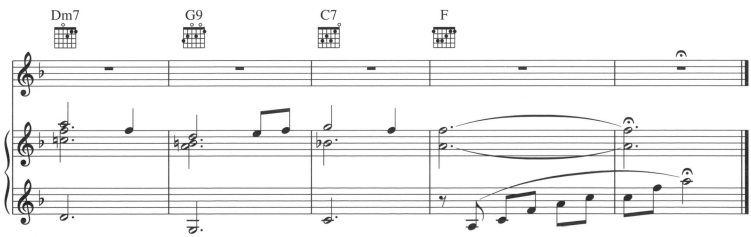

MY ATTORNEY BERNIE

Words and Music by
DAVE FRISHBERG
Arranged by DAVE FRISHBERG

Brazilian feel (in 2)

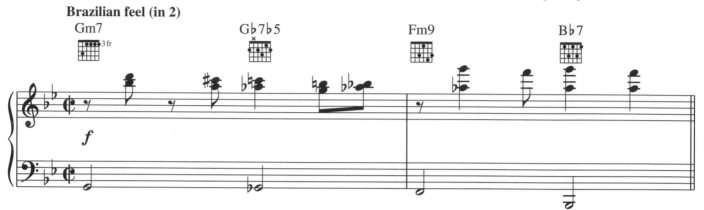

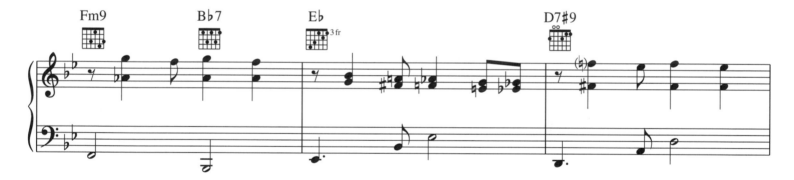

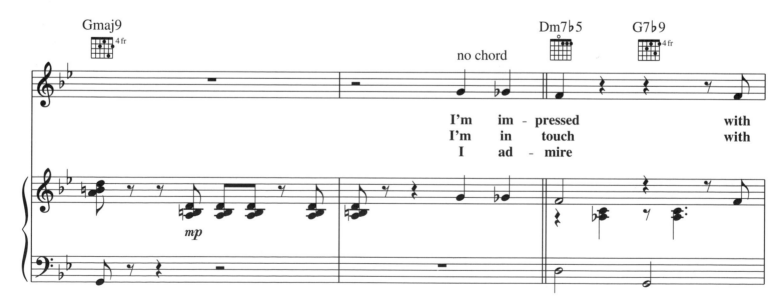

I'm   im - pressed   with
I'm   in   touch   with
I   ad - mire

sue, we ____ sue; Ber - nie says we sign,

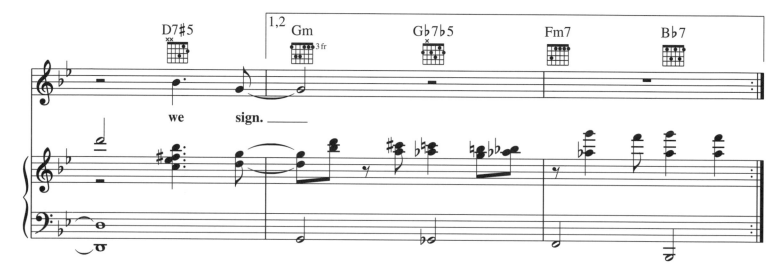

we sign. ____

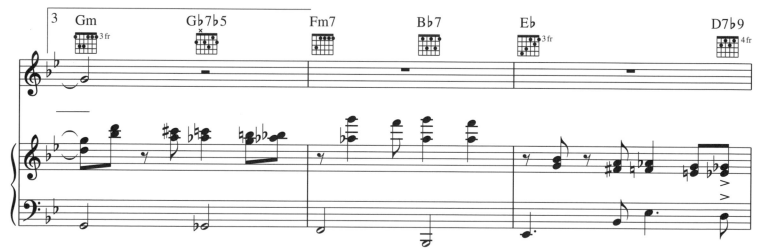

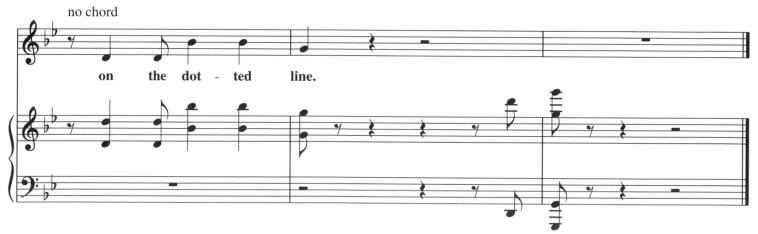

on the dot - ted line.

MY COUNTRY USED TO BE

Words and Music by
DAVE FRISHBERG
Arranged by DAVE FRISHBERG

once was proud. We stood a - bove the crowd.

No need to shout out loud, "We're num - ber one!"

Freely

I hope my chil-dren live to see a land like my coun-try used to

be.

MY SWAN SONG

Words and Music by
DAVE FRISHBERG
Arranged by DAVE FRISHBERG

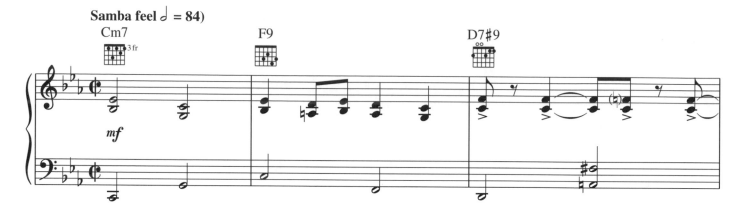

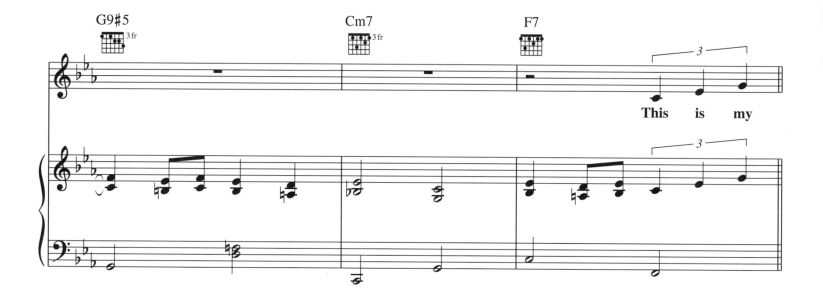

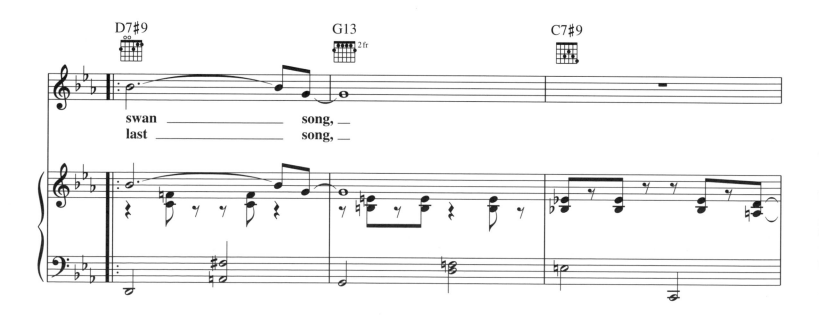

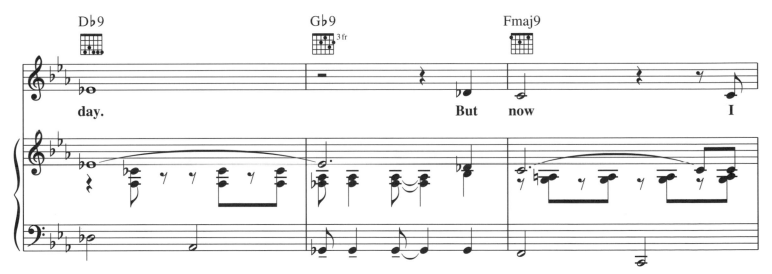

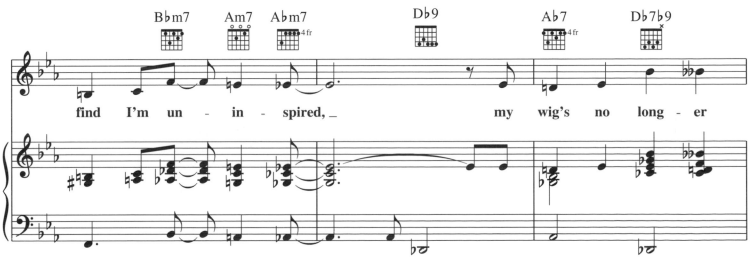

PEEL ME A GRAPE

Words and Music by
DAVE FRISHBERG
Arranged by DAVE FRISHBERG

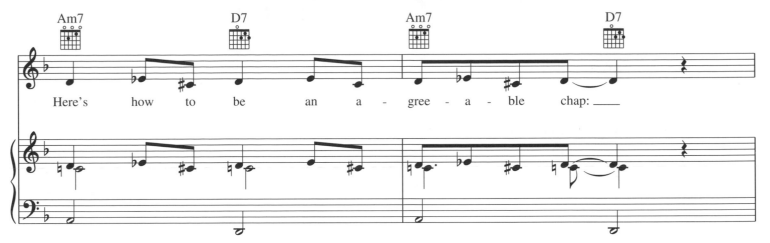

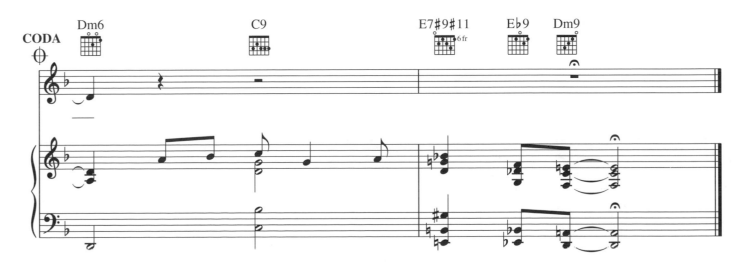

OKLAHOMA TOAD

Words and Music by
DAVE FRISHBERG
Arranged by DAVE FRISHBERG

OUR LOVE ROLLS ON

Words and Music by
DAVE FRISHBERG
Arranged by DAVE FRISHBERG

Ballad, not too slow

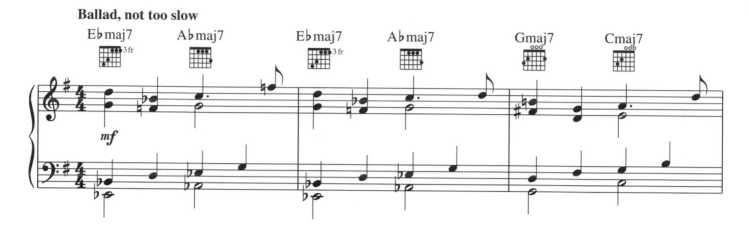

The clouds hang low, and the rains do fall, and

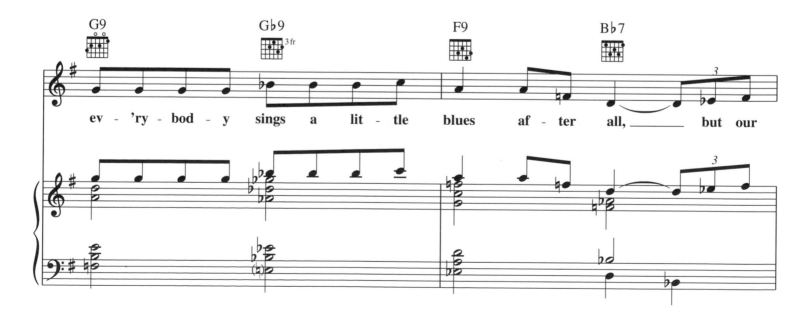

ev-'ry-bod-y sings a lit-tle blues af-ter all, _____ but our

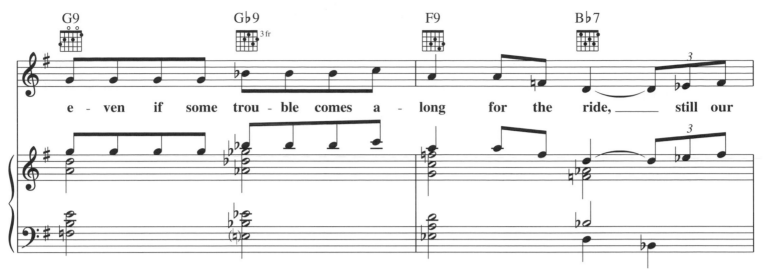

even if some trou-ble comes a-long for the ride, _____ still our

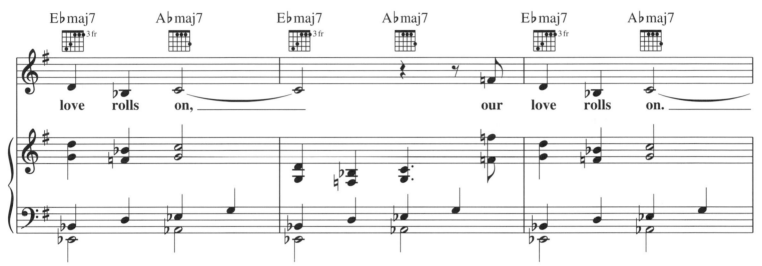

love rolls on, _____ our love rolls on. _____

We can rise a-bove it, 'cause our love rolls

rubato

on and on and on. _____

PLAY BALL

Words and Music by
DAVE FRISHBERG
Arranged by DAVE FRISHBERG

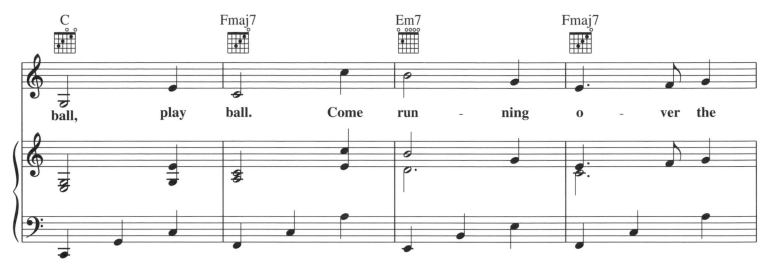

ball,   play ball.   Come run - ning o - ver the

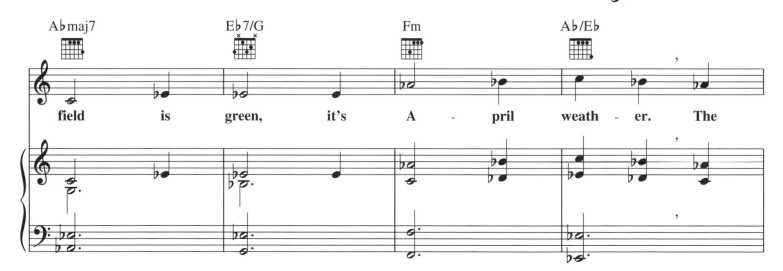

bare - foot clo - ver and join us there.   The

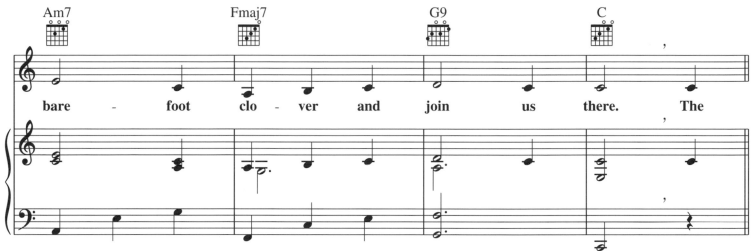

field   is   green,   it's   A - pril weath - er.   The

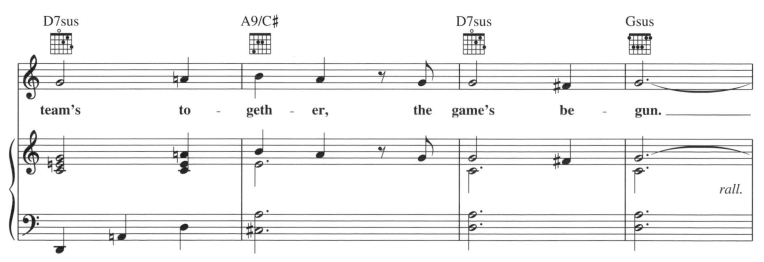

team's   to - geth - er,   the game's be - gun. _____

rall.

Play ball, play ball. Heads up now,

a tempo

lads, and we'll play it out 'til it's lost or

won.

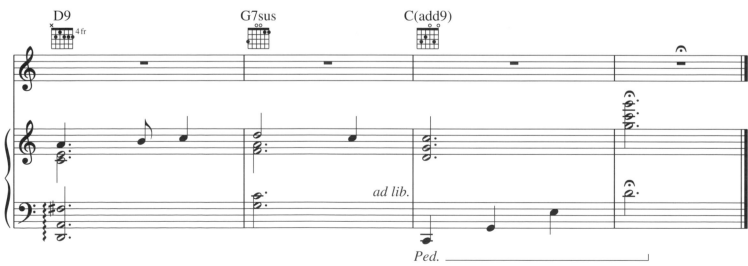

L.H.

ad lib.

Ped.

SARATOGA HUNCH

Words and Music by
DAVE FRISHBERG
Arranged by DAVE FRISHBERG

QUALITY TIME

Words and Music by
DAVE FRISHBERG
Arranged by DAVE FRISHBERG

I'll be late get-ting home from the of-fice, and so will you, 'cause we both got a mil-lion calls to re-turn, and a mil-lion things to do. We're not see-ing e-nough of each oth-er, 'cause truth be

SNOWBOUND

Words and Music by
DAVE FRISHBERG
Arranged by DAVE FRISHBERG

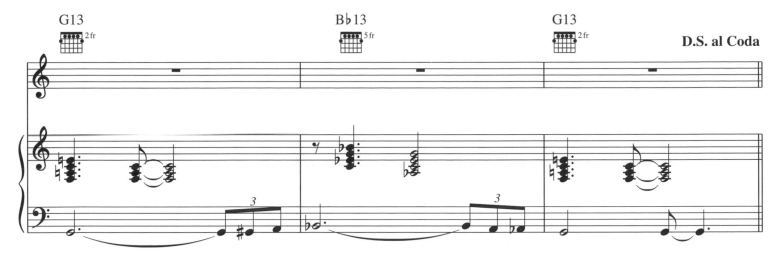

D.S. al Coda

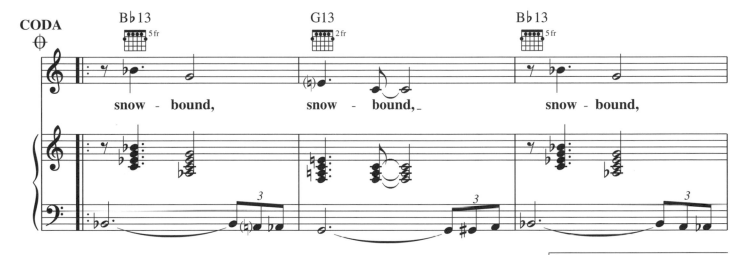

snow - bound, snow - bound, snow - bound,

snow - bound, snow - bound.

Just us two.
Me and you.

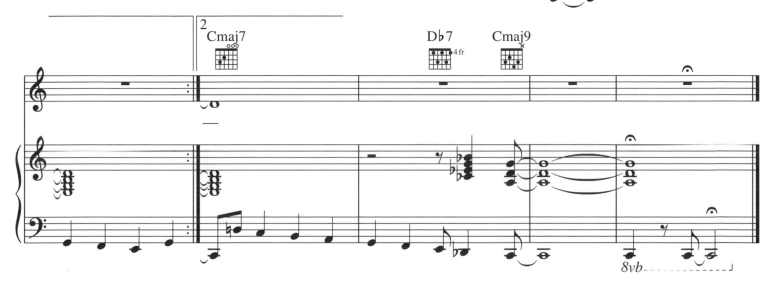

8vb

SWEET KENTUCKY HAM

Words and Music by
DAVE FRISHBERG
Arranged by DAVE FRISHBERG

YOU ARE THERE

Words by DAVE FRISHBERG
Music by JOHNNY MANDEL
Arranged by JOHNNY MANDEL

TOO LONG IN L.A.

Words and Music by
DAVE FRISHBERG
Arranged by DAVE FRISHBERG

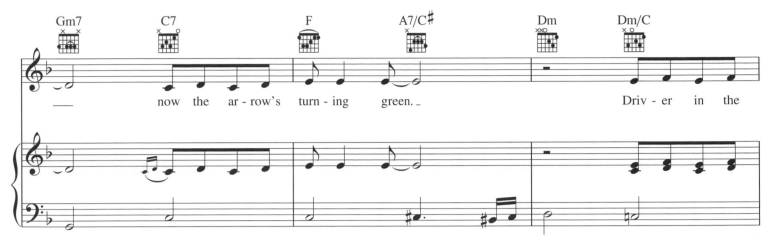

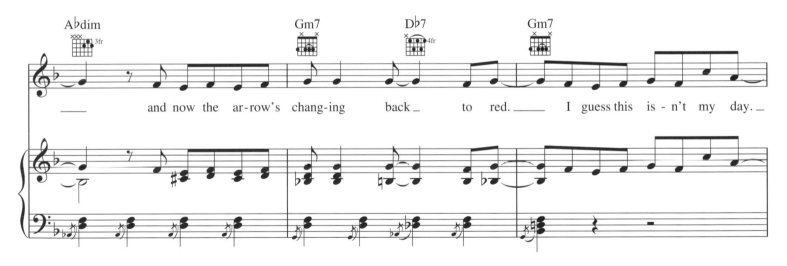

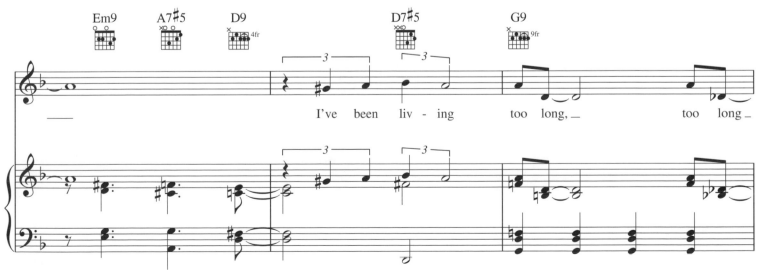

D.S. al Coda

in L. A.

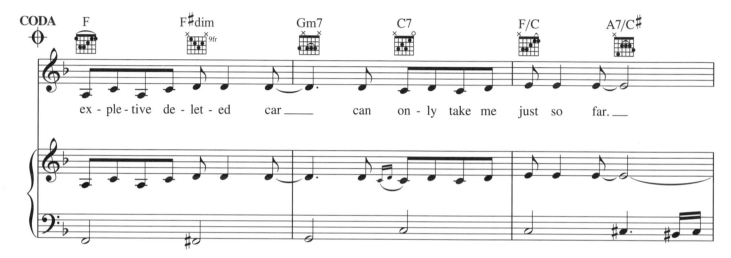

CODA

ex - ple - tive de - let - ed car ___ can on - ly take me just so far. ___

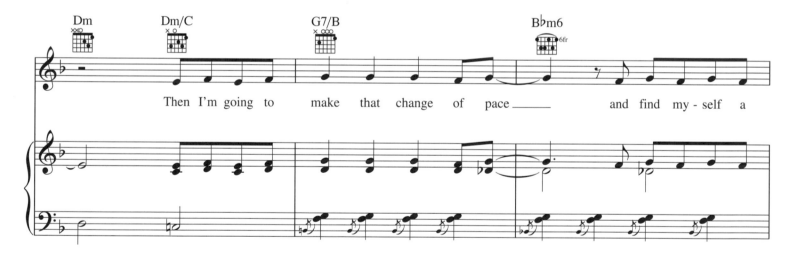

Then I'm going to make that change of pace ___ and find my-self a

pri - mo park - ing place. ___ And I'll be say - ing, "So long, ___ so long. ___

THE UNDERDOG

Words by DAVE FRISHBERG
Music by AL COHN
Arranged by DAVE FRISHBERG

VAN LINGLE MUNGO

Words and Music by
DAVE FRISHBERG
Arranged by DAVE FRISHBERG

Cos - ky, Hal Tros - ky...

Au - gie Ga - lan and Pink - y May,
John An - to - nel - li, Fer - ris Fain,

Stan Hack and French - y Bor -
Frank - ie Cro - set - ti, John -

da - gar - ay...
- ny Sain...

Phil Cav - a - ret - ta, George _ Mc-Quinn,
Har - ry Bre-cheen, and Lou ___ Bou-dreau,

How - ie Pol - let and Ear - ly Wynn...
Frank - ie Gus - tine and Claude _ Pas - seau...

Art Pa - sa -
Ed - die Ba -

THE WHEELERS AND DEALERS

Words and Music by
DAVE FRISHBERG
Arranged by DAVE FRISHBERG

Brazilian feel (♩ = 72)

Seems ____ like all the dream-ers ran out of
Sure, ____ it's lit-tle won-der we're in se-
Soon ____ we'll all be zoom-ing off for the

dreams, ____ and noth-ing feels ____ the same. It's such a
cure. ____ Just o-pen up ____ your eyes; it's like the
moon. ____ Like pi-o-neers ____ we'll roam to find some

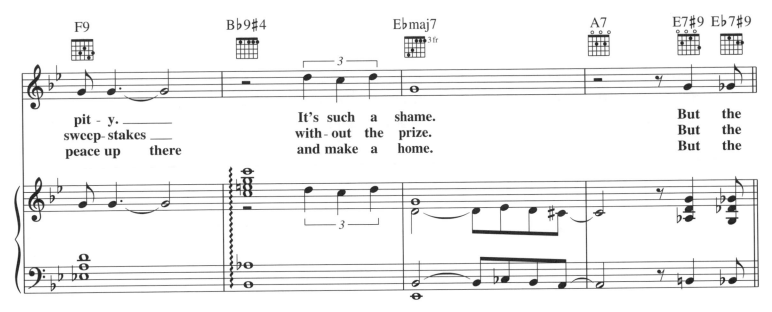

pit - y. _____
sweep-stakes ___
peace up there

It's such a shame.
with-out the prize.
and make a home.

But the
But the
But the

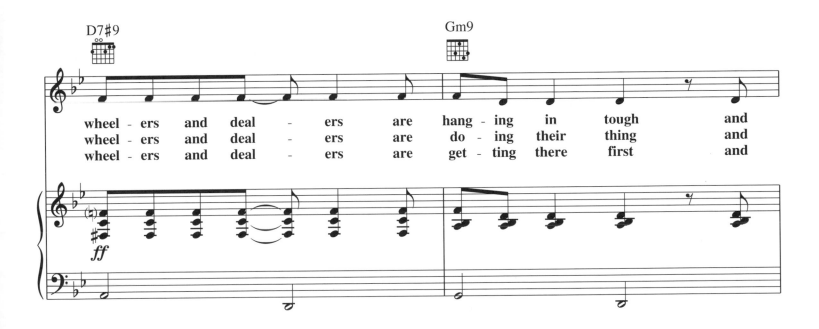

wheel - ers and deal - ers are hang - ing in tough and
wheel - ers and deal - ers are do - ing their thing and
wheel - ers and deal - ers are get - ting there first and

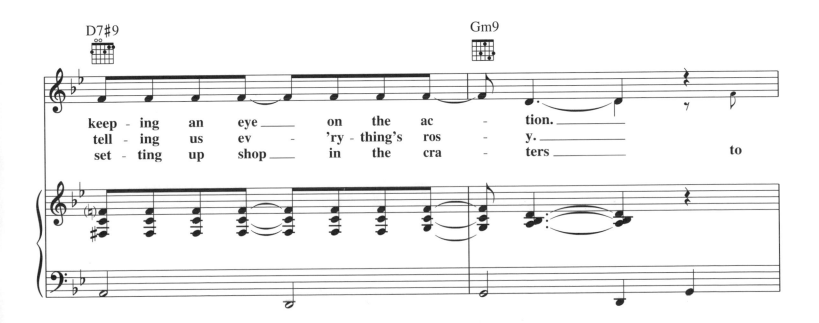

keep - ing an eye ___ on the ac - tion. _____
tell - ing us ev - 'ry-thing's ros - y. _____
set - ting up shop ___ in the cra - ters _____ to

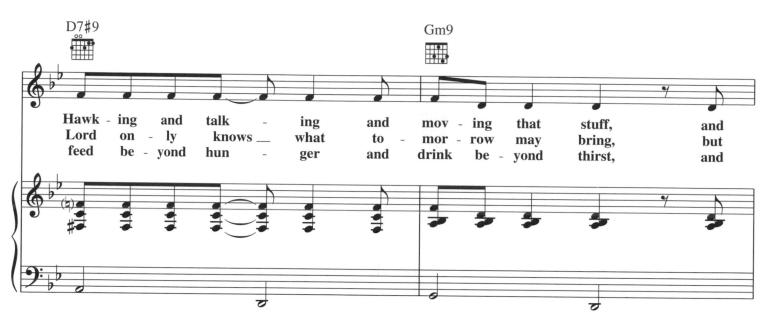

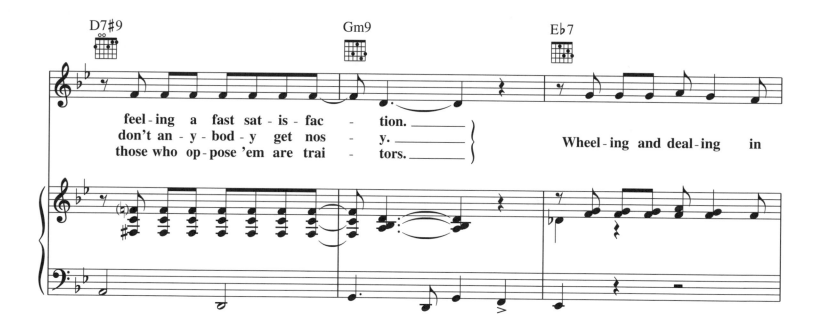

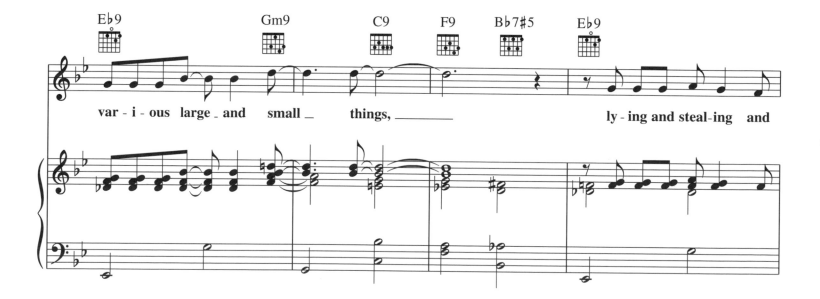

YOU WOULD RATHER HAVE THE BLUES

Words and Music by
DAVE FRISHBERG
Arranged by DAVE FRISHBERG

If ev-'ry wish you ev-er make at wish-ing well or wed-ding cake comes true, I feel sor-ry for you. And if at last your ship comes in, and fate de-cides to let you win the prize, I could hon-est-ly

float down from the sky, ___ you'd be known as the world's most luck-y guy. ___

An-y guy giv-en half a chance to choose ___ would choose ___

to be in your shoes. _____ But still ___ you'd lose, ___

no chord

To Coda

___ you'd lose, ___ 'cause you would rath-er have the blues.

ZOOT WALKS IN

Music by GERRY MULLIGAN and ZOOT SIMS
Words by DAVE FRISHBERG
Arranged by DAVE FRISHBERG

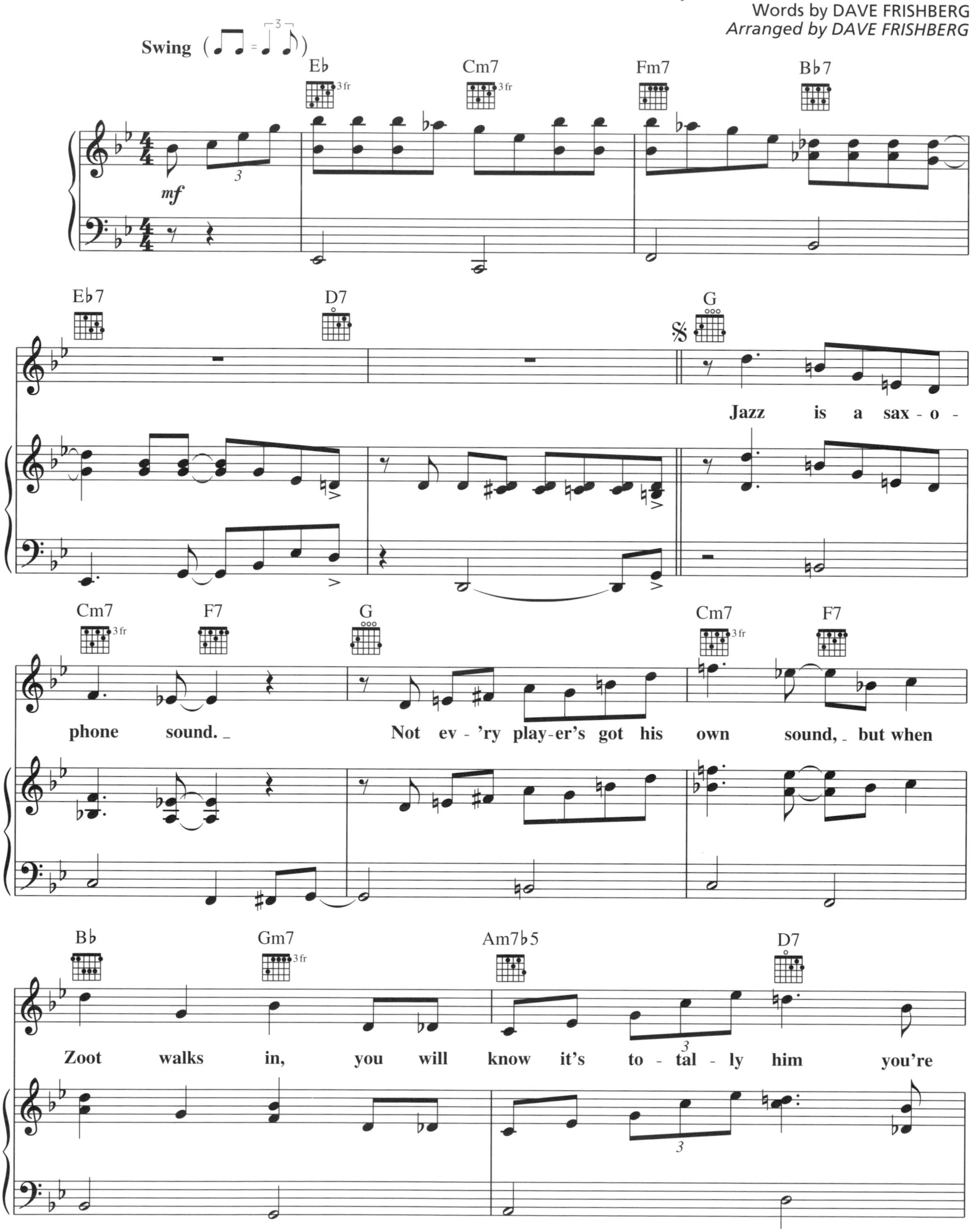

Swing
Eb Cm7 Fm7 Bb7
mf
Eb7 D7 G
Jazz is a sax - o -
Cm7 F7 G Cm7 F7
phone sound. Not ev - 'ry play-er's got his own sound, but when
Bb Gm7 Am7b5 D7
Zoot walks in, you will know it's to - tal - ly him you're

hear - ing. ___ Got a tone ___ all his own, ___ a hap - py kind of

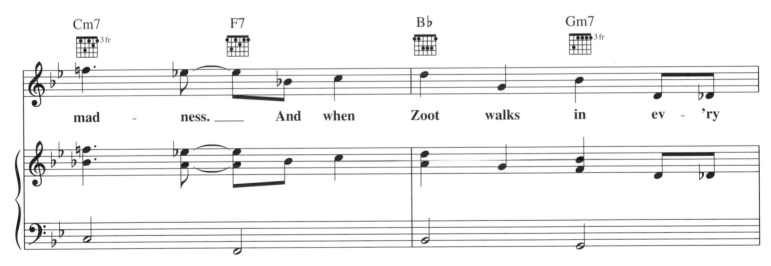

sad - ness, ___ with just a touch of ten - or

mad - ness. ___ And when Zoot walks in ev - 'ry

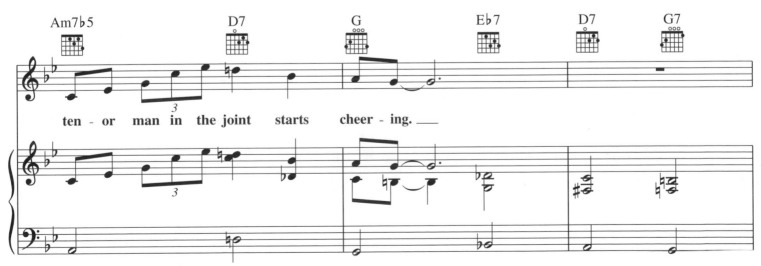

ten - or man in the joint starts cheer - ing. ___

ZANZIBAR

Words and Music by
DAVE FRISHBERG
Arranged by DAVE FRISHBERG

you may de - cide you want to

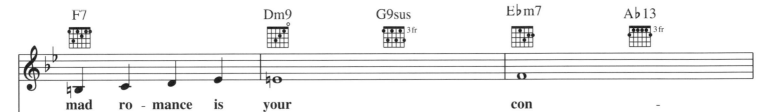

stay. ___ And if

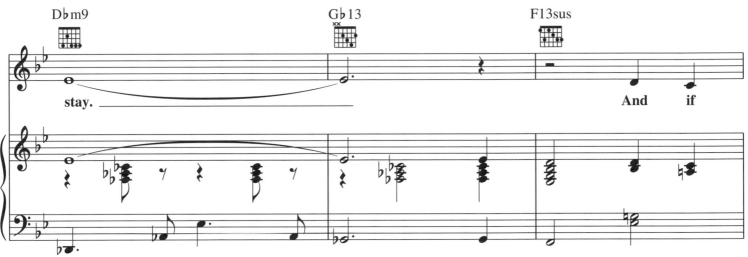

mad ro - mance is your con -

cern, you may nev - er re - turn ___